Where Children Grow

Wood Engraving of Friedrich Froebel, c. 1840
Artist Unknown

Where Children Grow

Wisdom for Raising Resiliant Humans
from the Inventor of Kindergarten

Friedrich Froebel

Edited by Miriam Mathis

Plough

Published by Plough Publishing House
Walden, New York
Robertsbridge, England
Elsmore, Australia
www.plough.com

Plough produces books, a quarterly magazine, and Plough.com to encourage people and help them put their faith into action. We believe Jesus can transform the world and that his teachings and example apply to all aspects of life. At the same time, we seek common ground with all people regardless of their creed.

Plough is the publishing house of the Bruderhof, an international Christian community. The Bruderhof is a fellowship of families and singles practicing radical discipleship in the spirit of the first church in Jerusalem (Acts 2 and 4). Members devote their entire lives to serving God, one another, and their neighbors, renouncing private property and sharing everything. To learn more about the Bruderhof's faith, history, and daily life, see Bruderhof.com. (Views expressed by Plough authors are their own and do not necessarily reflect the position of the Bruderhof.)

ISBN: 978-1-63608-138-0

Front cover image by Justine Maendel. Used with permission.

Selections from Irene M. Lilley's *Friedrich Froebel: A Selection from His Writings* are copyright 1967 by Cambridge University Press. Reproduced with permission of Cambridge University Press through PLSclear.

A catalog record for this book is available from the British Library.
Library of Congress Cataloging-in-Publication Data

   Names: Fröbel, Friedrich, 1782-1852, author. | Mathis, Miriam, editor.
   Title: Where children grow : wisdom for raising resilient humans from the
      inventor of Kindergarten / Friedrich Froebel ; edited by Miriam Mathis.
   Description: Walden, New York : Plough Publishing House, [2024] | Includes
      bibliographical references. | Summary: "A biographical introduction on
      Friedrich Froebel is followed by short selections from his writings on
      topics such as unstructured play, time in nature, creative
      self-expression, faith, sports, and building character"-- Provided by
      publisher.
   Identifiers: LCCN 2024010100 (print) | LCCN 2024010101 (ebook) | ISBN
      9781636081380 (paperback) | ISBN 9781636081373 (epub)
   Subjects: LCSH: Fröbel, Friedrich, 1782-1852. | Early childhood
                     education--Philosophy.
      Classification: LCC LB1139.23 .F76 2024 (print) | LCC LB1139.23 (ebook) |
                     DDC 372.2101--dc23/eng/20240412
            LC record available at https://lccn.loc.gov/2024010100
            LC ebook record available at https://lccn.loc.gov/2024010101

Contents

Foreword by Scott Bultman vii

Preface xi

Who Was Friedrich Froebel? xvii

1. Foundations   1

Reverence for Childhood   1

Guiding Children   6

Nature   10

Self-Directed Activity   16

Creativity   19

Play   23

Unity   28

2. At Home   31

The Parent's Task   32

Awakening Faith   41

Building Character   45

3. At School   55

The Purpose of School   57

The Role of Sports   58

Storytelling   61

The Teacher's Task   64

Bibliography 69

Notes 71

Foreword

MUCH HAS BEEN WRITTEN about Friedrich Froebel, the inventor of the kindergarten, since his death in 1852. His work was certainly known internationally during his lifetime, but his worldwide fame reached its peak in the early twentieth century, some fifty years after his death. At that time in the United States, his birthday was celebrated with gala affairs. Many major US cities had Froebel clubs or associations, fitting recognition for the man who gave the world the first successful form of early childhood education.

Why then have we forgotten Froebel? Was it due to anti-German sentiment stirred during World War I? Did the method become too diluted or rigidly applied? We certainly still have kindergartens in America, but they usually do not adhere to the child-centered, whole-child, play-based approach that Froebel pioneered.

My personal belief is that the shapers of our current educational system made a conscious decision to move away from Froebel. The Froebel kindergarten required well-trained professionals, and while early childhood education contributed greatly to the success of America's industrial revolution, the kindergarten was not easily mass-produced. As the demand for education increased exponentially, a lower percentage of instructors were properly trained and the application of Froebel's method became less effective. Educational leaders such as John Dewey, Patty Smith Hill, and William Heard Kilpatrick moved the country away from the kindergarten gold standard in the hopes of reforming Froebel's "romantic notions," bringing preschool education into the modern age. As a result, much of the real power of Froebel's approach has been lost.

There are echoes of Froebel's philosophy in the Reggio Emilia movement and the work of Maria Montessori and Rudolf Steiner, who both acknowledged him as an influence. While these adaptations of Froebel's work are not the original concept, they share his child-centered, whole-child, play-based approach. Such approaches in general have been relegated to the fringe by mainstream education, the legacy of Kilpatrick's published "critical" examinations of Froebel and Montessori. Kilpatrick's writings give a clear indication of how and why we abandoned Froebel's way for the promise of a more "scientific" approach.

The history of the Froebel kindergarten in America explains why the US education system finds itself in its current circumstance. The business of public education is finally collapsing under the weight of its own bureaucracy. The educational marketplace is finally driving a re-examination of educational methods as parents opt for homeschooling or the growing number of private alternatives. Will this produce better education, and most importantly, will the masses of American society be able to afford what really works?

Froebel education is still very much alive among the elite private schools of Europe and Asia. In the United States, a mystique has developed around Froebel's method, due primarily to its connection to Frank Lloyd Wright, Buckminster Fuller, and others. Increasingly, interest in Froebel education is based on a desire to help children develop as creative problem-solvers. The growing appeal of Froebel's ideas appears to be the result of a socio-economic shift that has been documented by Richard Florida, Daniel Pink, and Malcolm Gladwell. It seems that Froebel education may play the same role for the Technological Revolution that it did for the Industrial Revolution one hundred fifty years ago.

There are many today who claim to have the best interpretation of Froebel's ideas. He was not fully understood in his own time, even among those who spoke his native German. With so many passing years, it has become increasingly harder to find material about what he actually intended. Much of what is available in English was augmented by well-meaning followers. Perhaps the place to start is with his own words.

While there are several books attributed to Froebel, he himself authored only one book during his lifetime, *Die Menschenerziehung,* in 1826. Known today as *The Education of Man,* the title is perhaps more properly translated as "human education." Many of his other writings, including letters and articles from his weekly newsletter, *Das Sonntagsblatt,* have been published in books under a variety of titles which are attributed to Froebel.

It is important to consider Froebel's work as an educational philosophy more than a method. The power of his ideas is due solely to his emphasis on what we are as human beings. How can one properly develop a child without a clear understanding of human potential? The bulk of Froebel's material describes what we are: creative beings, co-creating within a creation. If this definition resonates with you, further study of Froebel education will be a rich and rewarding experience.

SCOTT BULTMAN
FROEBEL USA

Preface

GROWING UP IN RURAL NEW YORK, I enjoyed going
home with my two tree-climbing companions, because
their parents seemed unruffled by things like pine-pitch
hands or slightly torn clothes.

Lisa had discovered a method of climbing a white
pine's ladder-like trunk and then sliding down the outside
of the tree, branch to bouncing branch, which was a lot
of fun (and somewhat scary). Edith had a pet raccoon
she had raised. It searched her jacket pocket for apples
and rode her shoulder during our excursions. Saturday
mornings, I usually had to wait while Edith and Lisa
finished their chores around the house. Then we were free.
In our teens, the three of us built a log cabin.

I liked my friends' energetic mother, Annemarie, who
expected them to pull their weight at home yet supported
our enthusiasms. I knew she and her husband were
German; they had fled the Nazis on their honeymoon,
their daughters told me. But I learned only much later

that Annemarie had grown up in a village called Keilhau. Annemarie had been the only girl in the Keilhau boys' school where her father was principal – a school founded by a relative, Friedrich Froebel. (Froebel's niece, Emilie Froebel Barop, was Annemarie's grandmother.)

Edith and I were attending a teachers' college when she gave me these facts about her mother. While this connection delighted me, it was credible because Froebel had advocated just the sort of free play Annemarie had allowed her girls (and me, with them). He was the one who'd famously said that for a child "to climb a new tree means discovery of a new world" and considered the educator's role not as "teaching" but as accompanying children in their learning.

Although Froebel is best known as founder of the kindergarten, he started working with five-year-olds only after decades of teaching, so most of his ideas apply to children of all ages. He observed them closely, considered deeply, and recorded thoughts. Some of his longer works are not readily accessible, yet the more I immerse myself in them, the more I want to share what I unearth with teachers and parents. I love his image of the child as a flower, for instance, vulnerable yet strong. Take dandelions: you'll see them bloom in lush meadows or thrust through city sidewalks, in spring sunshine or winter wind. You will never change them into roses, no matter how you drench them with fertilizer. Determined and thriving, they remain what they were created to be.

Because Froebel honored differing learning styles, he particularly respected what he called self-activity. Rather than defining this term, I'll share an example from my own experience.

During recess one day, some of my fourth-grade students began damming the stream behind our school. No adult had organized this activity; it was their idea. Most people would call it play – but it was equally work, as the children exerted themselves to the limit, physically and mentally. Their first attempt failed, and they excitedly discussed possible reasons, probing in mud and water until they located and solved the problem. It took a long time. Up on the bank, another child was engrossed in a different world. Oblivious to her classmates' shouts, she carefully set acorn-cap dishes on a carpet of moss beneath overhanging tree roots. By the time I turned my attention elsewhere, she was perfecting interior decoration.

When I finally called my class back indoors, one of the dam-builders eagerly explained their project. He didn't seem to notice that his hands were cold and his sleeves wet. Nor did he realize that he and his friends had been experimenting with physics – and gaining skills in communication, teamwork, and troubleshooting in the process. But triumph shone from his eyes. The gnome-home designer said nothing, but she brimmed with quiet happiness.

Encouraging youngsters to discover their own solutions – to their own questions – was so revolutionary in Froebel's day that the state shut down his kindergartens toward the end of his life. Valuing initiative, independence, and imagination was countercultural in an era when children were meant to be seen and not heard. Industrialization had begun, and school was where the young learned to sit still and follow instructions.

What about now, two hundred years on? Have we lost Froebel's vision of childhood? From what I see and read, it seems that standardized curricula and testing, technology, and homework loads are robbing children of free play, the joyous self-activity and hands-on learning that rightly belong to education. Perhaps world leaders believe that accelerating children to academic success will secure their nation a leading edge in the world economy. But just as Froebel protested molding children like clay or stamping them like coins, we too can take a stand to protect children's right to a wholesome childhood. Peter Gray, a leading expert on the psychology of play, writes that today's children are suffering from play deprivation: "If we want children to reach their full human potential, we must accord them lots of freedom and time to play."

That's why I believe Froebel's reflections are as important in our day as in his. In compiling the following collection, I have combed his 1826 book *The Education of Man,* his autobiography, and other works – their English translations as well as the original German – for excerpts that I feel capture the heart of his message. In many cases, these have been slightly edited for clarity. I hope this book will encourage educators to step up in defense of children.

MIRIAM MATHIS

Miriam Mathis is a retired early childhood educator, German-English translator, and member of the Bruderhof.

Who Was Friedrich Froebel?

THURINGIA IS A STRIKINGLY BEAUTIFUL part of
Germany, and numerous poets, musicians, and philos-
ophers began life among its forested hills. Friedrich
Wilhelm Froebel, too, was born in Thuringia, in
Oberweissbach, on April 21, 1782. The famous Grimm
brothers – Froebel's contemporaries – collected folklore
in the neighboring region, and some of their bleaker tales
could almost have described his first years.

Froebel retained no memory of his mother, who died
before he was ten months old. His father, a Lutheran
pastor and strict disciplinarian, remarried when Friedrich
was four. After her own son's birth, the new mother spared
no love on her stepchildren, and Friedrich later recalled
that she treated him like a stranger.

"If anything went wrong while my stepbrother and I
were playing, I was blamed," he wrote. "Since our parents
assumed bad motives for everything I did, I became the
bad boy they thought me. Afraid of punishment, I began
to lie and deceive."

Friedrich occupied himself in the yard between
parsonage and church, with "only bugs and weeds for
friends." When he was old enough, his father sent him

to the local girls' school, its headmaster being a family acquaintance.

Circumstances changed for the better when Friedrich was ten, after a visit from his mother's brother. Sensing his nephew's loneliness, Pastor Hoffmann invited the child home with him, and for the next five years, Friedrich thrived on his uncle's trust. "My new life was vigorous and free. The world lay open, and I made the most of it."

Friedrich described the two parsons in his new village. "My uncle, the main pastor, conducted his life and calling with kindness. The second pastor was rigid, scolding, and commanding. The first led us with a glance; a word from him and few boys could disobey. The other's long exhortations went over our heads, immediately forgotten."

Similarly, he compared the two teachers at the school he attended with forty other boys. "One was pedantic and rigid. The other – our class teacher – was generous and free. The first had no influence over his class; the second we followed eagerly." Further describing this man's influence, Froebel wrote, "Our teacher's religious instruction confirmed my own thoughts, quickening and warming me. When he spoke of Jesus, my heart melted in longing for a similar life."

As these impressions affected Froebel's future course, so did his next chapter, when his father apprenticed him to a forester at age fifteen. As well as forestry, Friedrich delved into geometry, surveying, and agriculture, making full use of his master's library. Best, he spent hours alone among the mighty trees, where he marveled at nature's repeating patterns. He noticed, too, that trees damaged as saplings remained scarred for life. Applying this observation to children, years later, he wrote, "Education should initially consist in watchfully following, not dictating and interfering." Trees remained symbolic: "I would educate human beings with their feet rooted in God's earth . . . whose heads reach into heaven and there behold truth, in whose hearts earth and heaven are united."

After two years with the forester, Froebel pursued a range of subjects at the University of Jena, where botany studies reinforced his woodland observation that "everything strives toward unity." The romantic poets Goethe and Schiller also left their mark. But Friedrich ran out of money, and his two years at Jena were cut short by a stint in debtors' prison. He used the nine weeks for continued study.

Froebel spent his next three years doing clerical jobs on various estates. He hesitated over plans for the future, until, in 1805, he decided to train under a Frankfurt architect, supported by a legacy from Uncle Hoffmann. Yet doubt persisted. Would his architecture actually benefit humanity?

In Frankfurt he met a school principal, Gottlieb Gruner, with whom he shared wide-ranging discussions. After some weeks, Gruner suggested that Froebel, now twenty-three, drop architecture to teach in his model school of two hundred students. When Froebel agreed to give it a try, his passion was ignited. While teaching his first lesson to thirty or forty boys, he felt "as happy as a fish in the water or a bird in the air." He had found his vocation.

To his brother Christoph, Friedrich wrote, "From the first hour, the children were not strangers to me. I felt I'd been born for teaching. . . . This happiness comes both from my work's high purpose – education – and from the children's affection."

The school was based on Johann Heinrich Pestalozzi's principles, so Gruner lent his young employee a Pestalozzi publication. Reading it opened new realms of thought for Friedrich Froebel. "Pestalozzi's heartfelt goal was to build, in some corner of the world, an institution to educate the poor. This was oil poured on my spirit's fire. On the spur of the moment, I decided to visit this man." With Gruner's agreement, he set out for Yverdon, Switzerland, arriving in September 1805 after three weeks of walking. He was thrilled by Pestalozzi's school, where head, hands, and heart shared equal honor.

Back in Frankfurt, besides his teaching job, Froebel started tutoring three sons of a baron, von Holzhausen.

In July 1807, he left Gruner's school to focus on the von Holzhausen boys' education, setting two conditions: they would live with him in the country, and they would be entirely in his care. He now wrestled to create connection between academic subjects, believing that "joyful, unfettered work springs from perceiving everything as one whole." Baron von Holzhausen donated a field, where his sons helped their tutor tend plants they brought from surrounding hills.

Despite his zeal, Froebel felt inadequate to the task. So in 1808 he asked their father's permission to take the von Holzhausen lads to Yverdon for two years, certain both he and they would benefit from time with Pestalozzi. Froebel observed the boys' lessons, discussed their progress with Pestalozzi, and attended student teachers' lectures, which fueled his desire to continue working with children.

Even in Yverdon, however, Froebel sensed a disconnect between school subjects; when he and his students left, he was still seeking a more "natural, lively, and childlike way of teaching." In 1811 he enrolled in further university studies in Berlin, spending holidays with his brother Christian's family.

Froebel interrupted his educational pursuits in 1813. German-speaking states were joining forces against Napoleon's retreating army, and Froebel volunteered with the Lützow Free Corps. Enlisting connected him with two other students, Heinrich Langethal and Wilhelm Middendorf, with whom late night discussions kindled a lifelong comradeship. Their division participated in two battles, then disbanded when a peace treaty was signed in May 1814.

Following his military episode, Froebel returned to Berlin, where geology and crystallography classes had provided clues in his search for "the inner connection of the universe." In his new role, assisting at the mineralogical museum, ongoing study convinced him that all of nature – from snowflake to quartz crystal, pinecone to galaxy – follows related laws of growth and form. "Whenever I grasped this interconnection and unity, I felt my spirit's longing fulfilled," he wrote.

He turned down a professorship in mineralogy, though, because he'd come to believe that educating children could renew humankind. And he was convinced that all aspects of their education can be linked, just as divergent life forms connect.

In 1816, Froebel had opportunity to further test his ideas. His brother Christoph had died; and when Christoph's widow asked advice on her three sons' education, Friedrich offered to teach them himself, at their Griesheim home. His brother Christian sent his two sons as well.

Instead of conventional instruction and rote memorization, Froebel hoped for lively interaction between teacher and students – confident that when children's interest is kindled, they take initiative and "make the knowledge their own." His educational theories and method would keep evolving through time and experience, but his goal remained firm: that each child "understand himself, be at peace with nature, and be united with God."

"I would like to unite what I see divided. School and life must be one," Froebel wrote. He proposed that education should move outward from the familiar: from home, to school, to village. So he and his five nephews explored the area, drawing maps on their return. Froebel noted that the boys felt increasingly comfortable as they connected with their surroundings, with nature, and with other people. He respected them, and they in turn respected him and each other.

Froebel invited his two wartime friends to join the venture. Wilhelm Middendorf arrived at Griesheim in April 1817, bringing a sixth pupil.

Two months later, Froebel, Middendorf, and the boys piled their belongings onto a horse wagon, then walked beside it several miles to Keilhau, a picturesque hamlet of red-roofed, half-timbered homes clustered around the central church and fountain. In this typical Thuringian farm village, Froebel's school took root.

Honoring creativity as highly as academic achievement was almost unheard of. Yet Froebel believed that humans are essentially creative – and therefore children need opportunity to experiment and invent. He balanced morning lessons with afternoons of practical work, sports, handicrafts, art, and free play. Evenings were relaxed, with storytelling, singing, and hobbies.

Above all, Froebel hoped his students would be freethinkers. "Must we go on stamping our children like coins instead of seeing them walk among us as images of God?" was his challenge to other educators.

His own role was that of guide: attentive to – and building on – what inspired the boys. A wish from one of them to climb a nearby mountain for a birds-eye view of Keilhau developed into the first of many excursions. It was usually a child who called everyone's attention to a bird's nest or berry patch – confirming Froebel's claim that children heighten their teacher's awareness.

Heinrich Langethal arrived that September, as did more students. Within months, the number grew to fifty-six. Froebel drew floor plans and obtained permission to build a school. Construction began in November 1817, with teachers and boys helping the carpenters.

In Keilhau's woods and orchards, the boys gleaned apples, built fires, roasted potatoes, and cleared sledding tracks. They used materials from a torn-down shed to erect dens and forts; they reenacted battles and legends. If they had to be indoors, there were wooden blocks (and furniture) to build with. It was obvious to Froebel how much the children were learning – and how imagination blossomed – while they pursued their ideas. Why should school and play be separate? he asked.

September 1818 brought a big change. In Froebel's words, "I brought to the household – now so rich in children and brothers – its housewife, a lady to whom I'd been drawn by a shared love of nature and childhood, with high ideals for children's education." Froebel had met Henrietta Hoffmeister at university in Berlin, and she was thirty-eight when she left her affluent home to marry him and help realize their dream. She cheerfully accepted Keilhau's frugal lifestyle and loved the children as her own.

Prussian authorities became suspicious about this unusual school. In 1825 they sent an inspector, but he returned a glowing report:

> The institution presents a rare harmony – an intimate family of sixty, living peacefully, all doing heartily what they have to, with complete confidence in each

other, every member contributing his share, so that the work goes on of itself. The headmaster is loved by all.

Eighteen twenty-six marked publication of Froebel's most comprehensive and best-known work, *The Education of Man*. Its title would raise eyebrows today. So would its text, in which the author discusses "boyhood," "manliness," and "the boy." Readers must try not to trip over nineteenth-century gendered language (and bear in mind that Keilhau was a boys' school). Most of Froebel's ponderings apply equally to all children.

This book was Froebel's manifesto. As well as his belief that "Every life's purpose is to reveal God, through realizing its own nature," he wrote that each person is also a member of something bigger – a family, a community, a nation, the human race – and that wellbeing develops only in relation to the larger entity. "Children are like a tree's blossoms, manifesting humankind's ceaseless rebirth. As a bud is connected with the whole tree – root, trunk, branch, and crown, and so with earth and sky – so the individual shares life that is common to all."

Unity is the book's recurring theme: "Underlying the universal order of things is a living, all-pervading unity. This unity is God, in whom everything lives and has its being."

Unsurprisingly, the reactionary government continued to look askance at Keilhau. Following a crackdown on dissent in 1827, parents started withdrawing their sons from the school. From sixty students, the number dropped to five or six. The financial situation became dire.

After several years of hard luck and disappointments, Froebel consulted an acquaintance from his Frankfurt days. Xavier Schnyder, who admired Keilhau's spirit, offered a Swiss castle he owned. Froebel immediately set out for Wartensee Castle, hoping Switzerland would prove more tolerant than Germany. He hoped too that Keilhau School might fare better without him, since authorities there had labeled him a dissident. Schnyder arranged permissions, and the Wartensee School opened in 1831.

This venture soon seemed a false start, when Schnyder forbade renovations to the castle. Froebel and his colleagues were discussing their problems in a Wartensee tavern one evening when three merchants joined the conversation. On the spot, they offered another castle in nearby Willisau. Within days they had formed a union of twenty wealthy families who guaranteed support.

The Willisau School opened in 1833, with thirty-six pupils and several Keilhau staff. However, Froebel's assertion that children need no church forms – and his determination to protect them from "stony, oppressive theology" – antagonized Catholic Church authorities. "Hunt the wolves from the land, to the glory of God and the rage of the devil!" a Chapuchin monk incited the populace during a church festival.

On a local magistrate's suggestion, the teachers organized an open day, and a curious crowd arrived for the twelve-hour event, including authorities from Zürich, Bern, and neighboring cantons. Throughout the day, children answered questions so eagerly that onlookers broke into spontaneous applause. Shortly thereafter, the regional government, which owned the castle, reduced the rent – and banished Chapuchin monks from the canton.

Impressed by what they had seen on their visit, Bern authorities invited Keilhau staff to direct an orphanage in Burgdorf, where Froebel, Langethal, and their wives set up a day school as well, so town children and orphans could learn together. It was here that four- and five-year-olds were first included. When the local government had Froebel run refresher courses for teachers (in groups of forty), he became further convinced, through conversation with these colleagues, about the importance of including such young children.

Free from opposition for the first time in years, Friedrich Froebel enjoyed working with the Burgdorf children. His observations reinforced his certainty that time and space for free play are the best ingredients for wholesome development. In self-motivated play, children interact with their surroundings and find their place in the world, Froebel noted, and he described play as "free expression and activity of every kind."

During such play, children involved themselves with whatever materials were at hand, deciding what to do, how to do it, and meeting challenges that arose. Watching them, Froebel's respect deepened for what he termed "self-activity," implying involvement of the child's whole self: body, mind, and spirit.

This rewarding interlude was cut short when Henrietta Froebel became unwell and doctors advised leaving Switzerland. In 1836 the couple returned to Thuringia, settling in Blankenburg, four miles from Keilhau. In their rented house, a former powder mill, Froebel focused on caring for his wife, on production of his "gifts and occupations" (playthings he'd designed, such as cloth balls and wooden blocks), and on writing.

In Blankenburg, Froebel opened his first center exclusively for four- and five-year-olds. At the same location, he launched a course, in 1838, training young women and men "to take oversight of children before they are ready for school; to guide them according to their own natures; to help them develop their senses and physical abilities; to engage their minds; to acquaint them with the world of nature; to rightly guide their souls; to lead them to the origin of life."

Early the following year he spent time in Dresden, where a similar center was opening based on his principles. While there, he was invited to lecture in the palace, with the Queen herself in attendance. His ideas were gaining recognition.

Henrietta's illness worsened, and on May 13, 1839, she died. Froebel temporarily moved to Keilhau, to grieve his loss. But he knew his way forward lay with children, and in June 1840 he returned to Blankenburg to continue his work with four- and five-year-olds.

For a long time, Froebel had searched for a word to encapsulate his goals and values. In June 1840, he hit upon "kindergarten," and immediately knew he'd found what he was looking for. Often translated as garden for children, "garden of children" better conveys the word's meaning.

Froebel toured Germany with Middendorf, to develop more centers and teacher-training courses. In 1847 there were seven kindergartens, and forty-four more opened the following year. After one conference, attendees (some of whom had arrived skeptical) passed a resolution stating: "The Froebel school should form part of every child's education. . . . Teachers and educators present cannot withhold their approval from so excellent a system of training the young."

Despite his travel, lectures, and writing, Froebel still spent as much time as possible with children. He helped start vegetable and flower beds outside the Blankenburg kindergarten and wrote, "In their plots, children may plant what they like, how they like. In this way, they learn that plants must be treated with care." Noticing their pleasure in pushing his wheelbarrow, he composed a wheelbarrow song and had the local carpenter make forty child-size wheelbarrows.

In 1849, the Duke of Meiningen offered Marienthal Castle as a teacher training center. Froebel hoped it could also include a kindergarten, school, and orphanage, plus a workshop for design and production of educational equipment. He envisioned the Marienthal community as a model of harmony: between God and man, between people of all ages, and between each individual and nature. Reality fell short of his dream, however, and only the kindergarten and teacher training center came into being.

Louise Levin was a woman of wealth who had visited Keilhau in her twenties and later helped Henrietta Froebel in Blankenburg. Inspired to become a kindergarten teacher, she had attended the training course. In 1849 Froebel invited her help at Marienthal, where she became principal of the training school. And on July 9, 1851,

Friedrich Froebel and Louise Levin were married. He was sixty-nine; she was thirty-six.

Unknown to Froebel, renewed opposition had been mounting against his ideas. A month after the wedding, Karl Otto von Raumer, the Minister of Education, closed every kindergarten in Prussia. His stated reason: kindergarten was "part of the Froebelian socialistic system, calculated to raise our young people in atheism."

Froebel was sure there had been some mistake. With his goal of uniting children with God, how could he be considered atheist? And how could schools modeled on gardens be dangerous? He wrote to von Raumer, and to the king of Prussia, but to no avail. For a totalitarian regime, there was nothing more abhorrent than teaching children about freedom.

Froebel's disappointment was bitter. "As a machine of the state, I should have been engaged in cutting out and modelling other machines," he wrote. "But I only wanted to train up free, thinking, independent men."

Despite this blow – or perhaps because of it – he convened a three-day conference in September, attended by educators, church dignitaries, and government officials. As well as explaining his approach, Froebel led games with children, who were clearly enjoying themselves. At conference end, attendees praised the interaction between children and adults, as well as the gymnastics, artwork, stories, songs, and poetry. Froebel's courage was restored.

"I know it will be centuries before my views are generally accepted," he said, "but that no longer troubles me. If a seed has been sown, germination will follow, and so will good fruit."

Friedrich Froebel died at Marienthal on June 21, 1852. His approach to education was only beginning to receive wider attention. After his death, his views on childhood would gain momentum in England, the United States, and Canada (and more recently in Japan and South Korea), gradually reshaping education. "If three hundred years after my death my method of education shall be completely established according to its idea, I shall rejoice in heaven," he had written.

Froebel had always been an optimist. "I foresee a time, spread before my eyes like a spring landscape, when reverence for childhood and fostering creative activity – through which children give form to thought and internalize all they perceive – will convince everyone of the truth."

MIRIAM MATHIS

I

Foundations

LET US ABSORB from children's lives into ours that vital creative energy of childhood that we have lost. Let us learn from our children. Let us listen to the quiet demands of their hearts. Let us live for our children; then their lives will bring us joy and peace, and we will ourselves begin to grow in wisdom. [1]

Reverence for Childhood

THE SPIRIT OF GOD and of humanity – although as yet concealed and unrecognized – is revealed most purely and perfectly in each person as a child of God and of humanity as a whole if he unfolds and represents his own being as much as possible in accordance with his individuality and personality. [2]

EACH PERSON is a member of the human race in his or her unique way; the destiny of humanity – to be children of God – manifests itself differently in each individual. [3]

THE AIM OF ALL INSTRUCTION and training is the nurturing of each human being so that the inner and outer, the infinite and the finite, the eternal and the temporal are brought into living harmony. This nurturing should begin before birth while the parents await the child. [4]

THE CHILD must be accepted for what he is, what he has, and what he will become. [5]

WE GIVE YOUNG PLANTS and animals space, and time, and rest, knowing that they will unfold to beauty by laws working in each. We avoid acting on them by force, for we know that such intrusion upon their natural growth could only injure their development. Yet we treat the young human being as if it were a piece of wax, a lump of clay, out of which we can mold what we will. [6]

WE HANDLE CHILDREN so differently from other growing things. . . . Yet children proceed from the same source and follow the same laws of development as other growing things. Children are like varied flowers. They need care. Each is beautiful alone and glorious in community with its peers. [7]

FROM BIRTH children should be seen and responded to according to their unique nature, and given freedom for the many-faceted use of their powers. The use of particular powers should not be enhanced at the expense of others which are then hindered in their development. Children should neither be fettered nor given too much assistance. They should learn early how to find in themselves the center of their activity, and to move freely, to grasp with their own hands, to stand and walk on their own feet, to find and observe with their own eyes. [8]

AS THE GREATEST friend and loftiest teacher of humankind has said, the kingdom of peace and purity, unity and truth, belongs to the children, and only by returning to the spirit of childhood can we regain this kingdom. It is the return to childhood that ensures us those blessings of heaven, peace and purity, unity and truth, and all that of necessity blossoms and fruits from these; and it is the sanctifying and loving care of child-hood which alone can bring us earthly salvation and joy. [9]

YOU MUST KEEP HOLY the being of the young child; protect it from every rough and rude impression, from every touch of the vulgar. A gesture, a look, a sound is often sufficient to inflict such wounds. The child's soul is more tender and vulnerable than the finest or tenderest plant. [10]

ABSORBING A HOST of impressions through the senses is almost the only activity of infants. It is important that they absorb nothing morbid, low, mean, or ambiguous. The adults about them should be genuine, their surroundings firm and sure, stimulating confidence; the atmosphere should be clear and light-filled. The room should be clean, however modest it may be in other respects. Often the entirety of adulthood is not sufficient to amend impressions absorbed in childhood, simply because children's whole being, like a large eye, is open to them, wholly given up to them. For this reason the care of infants is so important. [11]

THE CHILD'S FIRST EXPRESSION is activity. . . . Children kick against whatever resists their feet; they seize whatever their hands touch. Soon after, or along with this, social feeling develops: hence the smile, the evident pleasure at moving their limbs in comfortable warmth, bright light, and pure fresh air. This is the first awaking of the child's human consciousness. [12]

THE FIRST SMILE, which instantly distinguishes
the young human being from any other creature, is
an essentially human characteristic, and certainly not
merely an expression of physical well-being. It is the way
in which the child first enters into communication with
other minds. [13]

TO SEE AND RESPECT in the child the germ and
promise of the coming youth and adult is very different
from considering and treating him or her as an adult
already. Parents who overlook this forget that they themselves became mature only insofar as they lived through
the various stages of their lives in natural succession. [14]

AT EVERY STAGE of development, the child, the youth,
the adult should be wholly what this stage calls for.
Then each successive stage will spring like a new shoot
from a healthy bud; it will follow that the individual will
accomplish what each stage requires. Only wholesome
development at each stage can lead to wholesome development at each later stage. [15]

OUR OWN HEARTS and our whole experience assure us
that only a very small part of what was lost in early years
can ever be ours. [16]

Guiding Children

WE FIND A FRESHNESS and richness in children who have been rightly guided and cared for in their early years. Is there any part of a person's thought and feeling, knowledge and ability, which does not have its deepest roots in childhood, any aspect of his future education which does not originate there? [17]

NO HIGHER JOY, no greater enjoyment can come to us from any source than comes from guiding our children – living for our children. [18]

TO BREAK A PATH toward the purest joy of life is not so difficult as you may suppose. But the truth whence such joy springs must live in you, and be the soul of all you do. [19]

IN EVERY ASPECT of training it is most important that the child's development be recognized as a steady evolution from stage to stage. It is most disastrous to act on the opposite theory – to divide the very marrow of life by marking sharp contrasts and setting definite limits between stages. . . . In real life, the stages – infant, child, youth, adult, old age – show an unbroken transition. [20]

IF I PIERCE the young leaf of the shoot of a plant with the finest needle, the prick forms a knot which grows with the leaf, becomes harder and harder, and prevents it from obtaining its perfectly complete form. Something similar takes place after wounds which touch the tender germ of the human soul and injure the heart-leaves of its being. [21]

LET US ALL be candid for once and confess that we feel mental wounds, which never heal while we live; hardened spots in our hearts that soften no more; dark places in our intellects that will never get bright; and all this because noble human feeling and thoughts natural to childhood were in our childhood crushed or lost, chiefly through early misdirection. [22]

WE DO NOTHING but harm – though we believe ourselves to be doing service to God and humankind, and especially to the child's own future good – by cutting off some of their natural tendencies and trying to graft others in their place.... God develops what is least and most imperfect, in steady progression, by eternal, self-evolving laws. [23]

TO TAKE ANOTHER EXAMPLE from nature – the grapevine must be pruned, but the pruning may destroy or impair the productivity of the vine if the gardener fails to follow the nature of the plant in his work. [24]

IF WE DO NOT FORCE nature or drive it in a direction opposite to its peculiar bent, if we recognize its general law and give each particular power its free development and all the support and care it needs, as an intelligent gardener does with his plants, the human powers will be better able to bring forth blossoms. [25]

THE MOST UNFORTUNATE CHILDREN are those whose untrained nurses or mothers foolishly do for them what they should do for themselves, and point out to them the things they should see for themselves. The child is seriously injured by such treatment. It trains children to believe that their function in the world is to demand and receive attention, and they inevitably become imperious, weak, and selfish. [26]

LESSONS THROUGH AND BY WORK, through and from life, are by far the most impressive. [27]

TO HAVE FOUND one fourth of the answer by their own efforts is of more value and importance to children than it is to half hear and half understand it in the words of another. [28]

THERE ARE MANY FAULTS which arise simply through carelessness. When children act on an impulse, they can become so entirely absorbed that they have no thought for the consequences, and indeed from their own limited experience can have no knowledge of them. [29]

CHILDREN ARE almost incredibly shortsighted in following their impulses. A boy will throw stones at a window quite intending to hit it, without considering that if he should succeed the window will break; and when the breakage actually happens he stands rooted to the spot in consternation. [30]

A LITTLE BOY by no means badly disposed once powdered with plaster of Paris the wig of an uncle of whom he was really fond. He quite enjoyed doing it, and never thought of the injury his joke might do to the wig. [31]

WHEN ASSUMPTIONS about children's attitudes are drawn from their behavior, widespread mistakes can be made. Many misconceptions arise and, as a result, parents blame their children or have foolish expectations. If parents and teachers are to establish secure and happy relations with children, they must try to act on this precept. The child who seems rude and self-willed is often involved in an intense struggle to realize the good by his own effort. The child who appears unresponsive may really be steadily intent on a line of thought that claims his whole attention. [32]

WHO CAN DOUBT that the child is satisfied with the joyful conviction that he has acted as his parent would wish, and has no thought of any extrinsic reward? We degrade human nature when we set up an external prize as a motive for conduct – even though that prize allures to a better world – and neglect to cherish the active spiritual force which urges every human being to a worthy human life. [33]

Nature

IF PEOPLE ARE TO FULLY ATTAIN their destiny, if they are to become truly an unbroken living unit, they must feel and know themselves to be one, not only with God and humanity, but also with nature. [34]

OUTDOOR LIFE, in open nature, is particularly desirable for young people; it develops, strengthens, elevates, and ennobles. [35]

FROM EVERY POINT in nature a road leads to God. [36]

THE DIVINE is not only in the greatest, it is also in the most minute things; in full abundance and power it is even in the least thing. [37]

AS HUMANITY in the dawn of its existence apprehended clearly the language of nature, so in the thousand voices of nature does the child hear God speaking to him or her. [38]

CONSEQUENTLY, PARENTS AND FAMILY should regard contact with nature as one of the chief moving forces of the life of the child, and should make it as full and rich as possible. And the best means is play, for play is the child's natural life. [39]

TEACHER AND PUPIL, parent and child walk always in one great living universe. The teacher or parent should never claim to know nothing of all this . . .

In order to know the unity that is within nature, there is no need of technical terms. Teachers should not think they have no knowledge of nature because they do not know the terms; they can learn far more from observation than from reading books. The so-called higher learning is usually based on observations that the simplest person can make if he knows how to use his eyes. He can make better observations than those achieved by the costliest equipment, provided he studies continuously and accepts the guidance of the children around him. [40]

PARENTS NEED NOT THINK that they cannot teach their children because they themselves know nothing; this may be so, but it is no great evil if they are willing to learn. You should become a child with the children and let yourself learn, as they do, from nature, who is our mother, and from the fatherly spirit of God manifested there. How else does anyone begin to teach? [41]

THE HUMAN BEING, especially in childhood, should become closely acquainted with nature – not merely with its details and forms, but with the divine spirit that is contained within it. The child needs and feels this deeply. Where this sense of nature is still unspoiled, nothing unites teacher and pupil so closely. . . . Teachers should regularly take their classes out-of-doors – not driving them out like a flock of sheep or leading them like a company of soldiers, but walking with them as a father with his children or a brother with his siblings and making them more familiar with whatever the season offers. [42]

WHERE POSSIBLE, grant your child the joy of caring for living things. [43]

CHILDREN SHOULD SEEK to determine to what extent the habitat and food of living things affect their color and even their form; how, for instance, the caterpillar, the butterfly, and other insects, in form and color, are connected with the plants to which they seem to belong. Children should not fail to notice how this external resemblance serves to protect the animals, and how higher animals almost intentionally make use of such resemblances; how, for instance, certain birds build their nests in trees whose color is scarcely to be distinguished from that of the nests; how, indeed, the color expression of animals harmonizes with the character of the time of day when they are most active, or with the activity of the sun – for example, the brilliant colors of butterflies and the dull colors of moths. [44]

LITTLE CHILDREN often ill-treat insects and animals without any cruel design, in a desire to get insight into their lives and to understand their spirits. If guidance and explanation are lacking, or if this impulse is misunderstood, it may in time harden into cruelty. [45]

IT IS PARTICULARLY IMPORTANT that children should cultivate gardens of their own, for there they will first see their efforts leading to an organic result. Children will see that the yield, though subject to laws of nature they cannot control, depends largely on the character of their work. Here their life with nature and their curiosity about flowers and plants and other natural phenomena will be fully and variously satisfied, and their efforts will be rewarded, for children's gardens usually grow and flourish. If children cannot have a garden plot of their own, they should at least have a plant or two in a box or pot, and these should be common and prolific plants rather than rare, delicate ones. Children who have cared for another living thing, even though it is of a lower order, are more easily led to care for their own life. The care of plants will also satisfy their desire to watch living creatures in other ways, for they will see birds and butterflies and beetles coming nearby. [46]

ANOTHER SIGNIFICANT DEVELOPMENT is the boy's liking for climbing into caves and crevices and wandering in dark woods and forests. He wants to seek out and find the undiscovered, see and know the unseen, uncover and possess that which exists in darkness. From such excursions he brings back rich spoils of unfamiliar stones and plants, of creatures that live in the dark – worms, beetles, spiders, lizards. "What is this? What is its name?" Every word that we give in answer enriches his world. What one must never do is to call out as he comes along, "Throw that horrid thing away," or, "Drop it, it will sting you." If the child takes notice, he rejects something essential to himself. Later on, when you or his own common sense tells him to look at a little creature which is quite harmless, he will look away and a great deal of knowledge will be lost. On the other hand, a little boy hardly six years old can tell you things about the wonderful organism and movement of a beetle which you have never noticed before. You should, of course, warn a child to be careful in handling unfamiliar creatures, but never in such a way as to make him afraid. [47]

WE OUGHT TO CULTIVATE intelligently children's observation of, and pleasure in, the moon, the night sky, and the stars. We ought to cultivate all this far more than we do . . . in order to excite, for one thing, a correct way of looking at and understanding the moon and the starry sky; as, for instance, the moon's spherical form, often so clearly to be seen; but, for another thing, to lead the children early on to feel, as they look at the starry sky, the being of its Creator. [48]

Self-Directed Activity

AN ETERNAL LAW pervades and governs all things. . . .
Each thing exists only because the divine spirit lives
in it and this divine spirit is its essence. The destiny of
everything is to reveal its essence, that is, the divine spirit
dwelling in it. It is the special function of man as an
intelligent and rational being to realize his essence fully
and clearly, to exercise, practice, and reveal the divine
spirit in him, freely and consciously in his own life. [49]

OUR PURPOSE is to make it possible for everyone to
develop from their earliest days freely and independently
as a whole person, as an individual being in harmony
with the whole of life. We wish to enable them to educate
and instruct themselves, recognizing and revealing both
their individuality and their part in the living universe. [50]

THE SPIRIT, not the external form, is the goal. The
life of Jesus, the highest and most perfect known to
humankind, found its fulfillment within its own being.
This perfect life would have each human being likewise
become a similar image of the eternal, developing from
within, self-active and free, in accordance with the
eternal law. This is, indeed, the aim of all instruction and
training; there can be no other. [51]

EVERY HUMAN BEING has one thought peculiarly and predominantly his own, the fundamental thought of his whole being, the key note of his life-symphony, a thought which he seeks to express and render clearly with the help of a thousand other thoughts, with the help of all he does. [52]

JESUS SAYS, "My meat is to do the will of him who sent me" – to work out whatever God has required me to do and as he has required it. Thus the lilies of the field – which in the ordinary human sense do not toil – are clothed more splendidly than Solomon in all his glory. But does not the lily put forth leaves and blossoms, does it not in its whole outward being reveal the inner being of God?

The birds of the air, in the human sense, neither sow nor toil; but do they not in their song, in the building of their nests, in all their varied actions reveal the spirit and life which God put into them? And God feeds and keeps them.

Thus people should learn from the lilies of the field and the birds of the air to reveal in their outer work and deeds the spirit that God breathed into them. [53]

THE GENUINE, VIGOROUS BOY is by no means always on the heights or in the depths. The same desire that urges him to seek knowledge and insight on the mountains and in the valleys, attracts and holds him also to the plain. Here he makes a little garden under the hedge near the fence of his father's garden; there he represents the course of the river in the fall or pressure of water upon his little waterwheel; here he observes a small piece of wood or a bit of light bark floating on a little pond he has dammed up. He is particularly fond of occupying himself with the clear, living, mobile water in which the boy who seeks self-knowledge beholds the image of his soul as in a mirror. For the same reason he is fond of busying himself with pliable substances (sand, clay), which to him are, as it were, a life-element. For he seeks now, impelled by the previously acquired sense of his power, to master the material, to control it. Everything must submit to his formative instinct; there in the heap of earth he builds a cellar, a cavern, and on top of it a garden, a bench.

Boards, branches of trees, laths, and poles are made into a hut, a house; the deep, fresh snow is fashioned into the walls and ramparts of a fortress; and the rough stones on the hill are heaped together to make a castle. . . .

Two boys, scarcely seven years old, with their arms around each other, walk across the yard in friendly,

intimate consultation; they are on the way to get tools
in order to build in a dark grove, on the hill behind the
house, a hut with a table and bench, a lookout from which
their eyes can take in the whole valley at one glance, as a
beautifully organized whole. [54]

THE CHILD'S KINGDOM may be only a corner of a
yard or house, perhaps only a box or cupboard, a den or
shed, but he must have some place to serve as a center and
point of reference for his activities, and this is best chosen
by the child himself. If the area to be controlled is large or
the project complex, this gives opportunity for a common
enterprise and, if the children all put their efforts into
it, they will enlarge the whole scope of the work in hand
or turn individual schemes into the basis for a common
activity. [55]

Creativity

UNLESS WE WOULD CRIPPLE our children's lives
both now and for the future we must educate them in
accordance with the demands of their nature. . . . We
must grasp children's earliest activities and understand
their impulse to make things and to be freely and person-
ally active; we must encourage their desire to instruct
themselves as they create, observe, and experiment. [56]

THIS CHARACTERISTIC of living and creative force, which is basic in humankind, is revealed in the impulse to create shape and form. It is seen in children's need to occupy themselves in observing things, taking them to pieces and then reassembling them. Children who are encouraged to do this find their needs fully satisfied and at the same time they are revealing their own nature. [57]

THESE ACTIVITIES are aimed primarily at the all-round development of the young human being. They are the food our spirits need, the air in which our spirits live as they grow in strength and scope. The qualities of mind and spirit with which God has endowed man unfold in all directions, appear in various forms, and must be met and satisfied in a variety of ways. [58]

GOD CREATES and works without end. Each thought of God is a piece of work, a deed, a product, and each thought of God continues to work with creative power to all eternity. [59]

SO PEOPLE, who have been made by God in his own likeness, should create shape and form. This is the deep meaning of work, of productive and creative activity. Through our work we become like God if, in doing it, we know or even vaguely feel that we are giving visible form to the spirit that is within us. Insight into the nature of God comes to us in our work. [60]

TO LEARN A THING through doing is much more developing, cultivating, and strengthening than to learn it merely through the verbal communications of ideas. Similarly, representing something by forming plastic materials, united with thought and speech, is by far more developing and cultivating than the merely verbal representation of ideas. [61]

THE WORD and the drawing belong together inseparably, as light and shadow, night and day, soul and body do. The faculty of drawing is, therefore, as much innate in children, in adults, as is the faculty of speech, and demands its development and cultivation as imperatively as the latter; experience shows this clearly in the child's love of drawing, in the child's instinctive desire to draw. [62]

A BOY has found a pebble. He rubs it on a nearby board and has discovered its property of imparting color. See how he delights in his discovery! Soon the whole surface of the board is changed. At first it was the color that excited him, but soon he takes pleasure in the winding, straight, or curved forms that appear as he works. In time he will represent a human figure through curves and straight and broken lines. Thus a new world opens within and without, for what people try to represent or do, they begin to understand. [63]

CHILDREN CANNOT SPEND all their leisure time in the open air, for seasons and circumstances may make it impracticable. Therefore all kinds of indoor occupations, especially constructive work with paper and cardboard, modelling and so on, should be included in their training. [64]

CHILDREN'S POWER to create is still limited. They should not, however, be prevented from using it; if they are properly educated they will always feel that their capacity is adequate to their aim. Their limitations serve to strengthen their desire by challenging their power, so they must not be disturbed in their attempts, however fruitless those seem to be, for their power to create is increasing. [65]

THE WHOLE NATURE of the parents' love for the child is shown in their concern to encourage and develop his or her creative impulses. We must regard people throughout their lives as creative beings and enable them to work independently. [66]

SINGING, DRAWING, PAINTING, and modelling at an early stage must, therefore, be taken into account in any comprehensive scheme of education; the school should treat them seriously and not consider that it is a matter of mere whim. The aim is not to make each pupil proficient in one or all of the arts – though in a sense this is true – nor to turn them all into artists, but to enable every person to develop all sides of his or her nature, while recognizing human abilities in their full diversity and appreciating true artistic achievement. [67]

Play

EVEN IF I HAVE DISCOVERED nothing new in children's education – as some people claim – I have made an important contribution by insisting on time for play. It is in play that children's energies can flourish, neither strained by too-early lessons nor rusting through lack of use. [68]

PLAY IS THE HIGHEST EXPRESSION of human development in childhood, for it alone is the free expression of what is in children's souls. . . . It gives them joy, freedom, contentment, and peace with the world. Children who play well of their own accord, quietly persisting until they are physically tired out, will develop as efficient and determined individuals, ever ready to make sacrifices for the good of themselves and others. There is no lovelier sight than that of a child absorbed in play. . . .

Childhood play is never trivial; it is deeply significant. Parents need to cherish and encourage it, for in their free choice of play children reveal the future life of their mind to anyone who has insight into human nature. [69]

THE FORMS OF PLAY at this age are the core of a child's whole future, since in them the entire person is developed and revealed in the most sensitive qualities of his mind. A person's life to its very end has its sources in this period when it is determined whether it shall be rich or poor in achievement, and whether he will be gentle or violent, show apathy or intelligent insight, create or destroy. His connections with family and society, with nature and God, all depend on his mode of life at this time when these relationships are in complete unity. So it is that he scarcely knows which he likes best – the flowers, his own delight in them, his parents' pleasure when he presents them, or his vague intuition of God who gave them. [70]

THE DEGREE OF SATISFACTION experienced in play determines the style and character of a child's future life. If this contentment is deeply grounded, other blessings of life will follow. It is a particular purpose of play to give such contentment and stability to the child. [71]

PEOPLE THINK children are only seeking amusement when they play. That is a great error. Play is the first means of development of the human mind, its first effort to make acquaintance with the outward world, to collect original experiences from things and facts, and to exercise the powers of body and mind. [72]

PLAY IS THE GREAT GAME of life itself in its beginnings. Hence the intense seriousness often observed in the attitude of children at play. [73]

WHAT BUSY TUMULT among those older boys at the brook down yonder! They have built canals and sluices, bridges and seaports, dams and mills, each one intent only on his own work. Now the water is to be used to carry vessels from the higher to the lower level, but at each step of progress one trespasses on the limits of another realm, and each one equally claims his right as lord and maker, while he recognizes the claims of the others. What can serve here to mediate? Only treaties, and, like states, they bind themselves by strict treaties. Who can point out the varied significance, the varied results, of this play of boys? Two things, indeed, are clearly established which proceed from this spirit of boyhood: the playing boys will make good pupils, intelligent and quick to learn, quick to see and to do, diligent and full of zeal, reliable in thought and feeling, efficient and vigorous; and those who have played thus are efficient men, or will become so. [74]

PLAY, THEREFORE, must not be left to chance. Because they learn through play, children learn willingly and learn much. So play, like learning and activity, has its own definite period of time and it must not be left out of the elementary curriculum. [75]

WHAT CHILDREN IMITATE they begin to understand. Let them represent the flying birds and they enter partially into the life of birds. Let them imitate the rapid motion of fish in the water and their sympathy with fish is quickened. Let them reproduce the activities of farmer, miller, or baker and their eyes open to the meaning of such work. In a word, let them reflect in their play the varied aspects of life and their thought will begin to grapple with the significance of each. [76]

THREE TYPES OF FREE PLAY occur during this period: children imitate real-life scenarios, they reenact what they're learning in school, and they engage in spontaneous open-ended play, pursuing their plans with all kinds of materials – inspired by the materials themselves or by some idea hatching from within. Whatever the type of play, their activity flows from their inborn energy and enthusiasm. [77]

DO NOT DISTURB children's free play. You would do better to look the other way, unless you can enter into the spirit behind it. In their play they are not dragging what is holy in the dirt; no, their play is a seed, a way of grasping for life's meaning. How can children learn to cherish what is holy, both now and throughout life, if you do not allow them free expression in innocent play? They should be able to express what comes from their heart without being disturbed by an uncalled-for look or comment. [78]

LET THE WORLD LAUGH at me now as much as it likes for my insisting upon and arranging children's play; it will one day acknowledge that I am right. [79]

Unity

IT IS MY FIRM CONVICTION that anything that
consistently makes children glad – anything that gives
them pure joy in life and a happy, sensitive soul, anything
where innocent laughter prevails – has an underlying
purpose leading upward to God. [80]

IN MY TENTH AND ELEVENTH YEARS, I came to
dream of life as a connected whole. . . . The silent longing
of my heart, the mainspring of my existence, was to find
everywhere life, harmony, and freedom from contra-
dictions, and so to recognize with a keener and clearer
perception the life-unity after which I dimly groped. [81]

THE MOST PRESSING THOUGHT which arose in me
was this: all is unity, all rests in unity, all springs from,
strives for, and leads to unity, and returns to unity at
last. . . . But a great gulf lay between my inner vision and
my outer perception, presentation, and action. [82]

THE CHILD EXPRESSES GOODNESS of heart and
mind in an intense longing to find in apparently separate
things an essential unity, such as he feels within himself.
In childhood this longing finds satisfaction in the full

enjoyment of play – for in play all things are related
to him and his life. This sense of unity is the primary
condition of all human development, and any feeling of
separation frustrates it. [83]

2

At Home

HOLD HIGH THE IDEA of the family as a holy thing, for in it lies and germinates the weal of all nations, the salvation of humankind. [84]

THE PRICELESS BLESSING of a happy home can be won only by struggle, endurance, and self-sacrifice. [85]

THE FAMILY is the place where understanding of the higher values of life should be fostered. . . . In the family, children should be regarded as an enrichment. [86]

WHAT IN REALITY is the birth of a child? An invisible spiritual being that has an eternal existence makes its appearance . . . Therefore, the birth is awaited with hope and joy, for the parents are filled with the idea that an eternal being is coming into finite existence. It is like the dawn of a morning that promises a clear, sunny day. The joy that pervades the whole family is based on the feeling that once again a phenomenon that begins to reveal the high nature of humankind has entered into existence. [87]

IN A FAMILY, children fully express the essential character of the whole – which may be quite unknown and so far unsuspected by it – if each grows to the full development of all his or her powers and yet does so in the most deeply individual and personal way. [88]

The Parent's Task

IT IS A GREAT and eternal truth that the relationship between God and man is mirrored in human relationships, especially in that between parent and child. [89]

PARENTS OUGHT to be pure and clean in word and deed, to be filled with a sense of human worth and dignity, to consider themselves guardians of a gift of God. [90]

EVEN AS A CHILD, every person should be viewed and treated as a necessary, essential member of humanity; therefore, as guardians, parents are responsible to God, to the child, and to humanity. [91]

CHILDREN ARE VERY IMPRESSIONABLE. Small, seemingly insignificant episodes in early childhood can do enormous damage to the child's future upbringing. If only we could forewarn each new young couple!

The feeling with which children are first welcomed should surround them always and should lead to careful observation of the way in which they develop and express their thoughts. So Mary from the beginning related everything to the higher spiritual life which was to come into existence through her, and so it is said of her that she kept all these things and pondered them in her heart. [92]

CHILDREN NEED ENCOURAGEMENT as growing plants need warmth and light, and they must have their parents' love and understanding. [93]

I URGE YOU to foster every breath of song in your family; children's song is to the family what the song of birds is to the leafy grove. [94]

THE FIRST IMPRESSIONS which a young child receives are stronger and more lasting than those in later life, because the power of resistance that consciousness later brings is lacking. As the thriving of the child's body depends in a great measure upon breathing pure air, so the purity and morality of the soul depend partly on the impressions which the baby and child receive. The careful nursing of the spiritual life must begin much earlier than the expression of it is possible. . . . This tender suscepti-bility requires a tender handling, or it is in a certain sense choked, as if I should cover the growing roots of this little plant I have here with sand. No development can be forced – not in nature, still less in the human mind. With right care, everything blossoms in its own time. [95]

THE DESTINY of nations lies far more in the hands of women – the mothers – than in the possessors of power. [96]

WHAT IS THE SUPREME GIFT you would bestow on the children who are the life of your life, the soul of your soul? Would you not above all other things render them capable of giving nurture? Would you not endow them with the courage and constancy which the ability to give nurture implies? [97]

IT IS A BLESSING for an infant's whole future when the mother lays him or her down to sleep with a prayer in her heart to their heavenly Father for protection and loving care. It is also highly important and full of blessing for the present and later life of the child when, with joy

and gratitude to God, the mother lifts the awakened
child from the crib. These experiences exert the happiest
influence. . . .

Children thus cared for by their mothers are well
conditioned in their point of view toward earthly, human,
and heavenly matters. Prayer gives peace; through God
one rests in God, the beginning and end of all created
things. [98]

EVERY EXTERNAL OBJECT comes to children with the
invitation to determine its nature and relationships. Their
senses enable them to meet this invitation. [99]

FROM A VERY EARLY PERIOD, children should
never be left too long to themselves on beds or in cradles
without some external object to occupy them. . . . In
order to avoid leaving children on their beds mentally
unoccupied while going to sleep, and still more, just
after waking, it is advisable to suspend in a line with the
child's natural vision, a swinging cage with a lively bird.
This secures occupation for the senses and the mind,
profitable in many directions. [100]

NOTE THE PECULIAR INTENSITY with which very
small children focus their eyes on objects that are new

or strange to them, especially if they are shiny or colored objects. Notice how much questioning, examining, weighing and comparing is expressed in the child's gaze. Yet this is not the effect of an impression of something strange and unknown, but rather a sign of intense mental activity. [101]

TRUE, INFANTS LACK the adult's power of deductive thought, yet they have a certain spontaneous insight and judgment, an immediate response, which is for that very reason all the more likely to be right. . . . Babies may appear helpless but their power of thought is much greater than we imagine. [102]

CHILDREN ARE INTENSELY ACTIVE and continuously occupied, and they are hurt if their plaything is taken away too soon. It is good for children to concentrate on an object, on a series of mental pictures, for they often need to be occupied for a long time with some quite simple thing. So we ought not to distract their attention or try to take an object away from them or regard them as destructive if they soon throw everything away. [103]

THE SIMPLE, natural mother carefully follows the slow but complete development of her child's life. She instinctively tries to incite all his or her limbs and senses to full activity, and so stimulates to ever-increasing activity the yet richer inner life, and by such activity develops it. [104]

YOUR CHILD will begin to imitate you, for whatever mother loves a child gladly repeats. This imitative activity should be carefully cultivated. Rightly directed, it will lighten by more than half the work of education. Utilized at the proper stage of development, it will enable you to accomplish by a touch as light as a feather what later you cannot do with a hundredweight of words. [105]

A CHILD SHOULD STAND when he is strong enough to keep his balance independently; he should walk when he can keep his balance when moving forward. He will rejoice greatly in the strength in his own feet and will repeat the art of walking for its own sake, as formerly he repeated standing. In a short time he walks without effort and is attracted by objects that now he can attain by himself – bright leaves, building blocks – and he tries to bring these things together. [106]

ALL THESE MATERIALS must be known, not only by name but also by qualities and uses; that a child desires this is shown in his quiet activity. How can we impart language to the things of a child's life, since in our adulthood we are dully uncomprehending? Yet it is the intense desire for this that urges children to bring their treasures to us. Children love all things that enter their small horizon and extend their little world. To them the least thing is a new discovery. A child wants to know why he loves this thing; he wants to know its properties. He examines it on all sides, he tears and breaks it, he puts it in his mouth and bites it. He wants to know the inner nature of the thing; an innate instinct which, properly guided, would seek to find God in all his works, urges the child to do this. [107]

YOUNG CHILDREN do not make a distinction between an object and its name. They do not separate body from spirit, as can be seen in their play. They impart to each pebble, plant, or animal the same faculties of life and speech they enjoy. Play and speech go together, and how very much they talk as they play! For them, their parents, the realm of God and the angels, and particularly the world of nature have the same life which they feel within themselves. Life with and in the fair, silent things of nature should be fostered by parents as a wellspring of a child's life. [108]

IT IS NOTICEABLE that the more the parent's talk touches the child's consciousness the more intensely is the child's inner life aroused, though the child still has limited means of expression. In his soul the child wants to break the barriers put up against him and he is impatient at this inability to communicate. [109]

WITH THE HELP of our explanations, children learn almost without effort. How little is needed from adults to aid childhood in this tendency to learn! It is only needful to designate, to name, to put into words what the child does, sees, and finds. [110]

LITTLE CHILDREN often sing to themselves when quiet, especially when going to sleep. Those who have charge of children should attend to and develop this, as the rudiments of a sense of melody and power of song. Were this done, a disposition for melody would soon show itself as it does at present for language. [111]

AS THEY GROW, children have a great desire to share in their parents' work. They do not want the easy occupations but the hard work that demands strength and exertion. It is at this point that parents need to be careful and sensible. By rejecting their children's help as useless and even obstructive they could suddenly destroy or dam up their children's creative impulses. Parents should never say, "Go away, you are only hindering me." Or "I am in a hurry and will do it more quickly on my own." Children who are interrupted in this way are disconcerted if they are excluded from the activity with which they had felt identified. They feel isolated and have no idea what to do with the energy that has been stimulated and is now only a burden. So they lapse into dullness and apathy. This rejection by the parents need only happen a few times and the child no longer offers to help or share in any work; he stands around listless and bored, even when it is work in which he could quite easily participate. So we hear parents saying, "Look at him! When he was small and couldn't help me he was always in the way, but now he just won't do anything." [112]

CHILDREN DO NOT ASK, or consider, why their help was at one time useful and at another time useless; they choose the easiest way, and give up caring to be useful. . . . Therefore, if parents wish for their children's help hereafter, let them early on cherish their children's active instincts, and especially this formative impulse of childhood. Even if it costs the child a little self-command and sacrifice, like good seed in good soil it will bring forth a hundredfold. [113]

A BOY WANTS TO SHARE the household labor – to be lifting, drawing, carrying water, splitting wood. He wants to try his own strength on everything, that his frame may grow stronger, and that he may know what he can do. The boy follows his father everywhere, into garden, field, and wood, goes with him into the workshop, tends the animals, or mends the tools, sharing whatever the father has to do. Question upon question springs from the boy's heart, which is thirsty for knowledge. How? Why? When? Whence? What for? And any tolerably complete reply opens up to the boy a new world; speech brings him into touch with all things. [114]

Awakening Faith

HARMONY IN FAMILY LIFE is the deepest root of genuine faith. [115]

FAITH IN GOD is innate in every person, every child. It has only to be awakened; but it must be awakened or it remains dead. [116]

WHEN A CHILD has grown up in true unity of life and feeling with his parents, this unity will be strengthened if nothing intervenes to disturb it. This spiritual unity, which is more than the vague feeling that arises from merely living together, is the firm basis of true religious sentiment. [117]

A SENSE OF COMMUNITY is the first beginning of all true faith, of all genuine striving for unimpeded union with the eternal. If faith is to live and endure, it must come to a person in early childhood when the innate divine spirit is yet dimly aware of its origin, and this obscure awareness must be fostered and strengthened in the child so that later in life he or she may clearly apprehend it. [118]

THE FIRST GROUNDWORK of faith is love – love to God and man – in the bosom of the family. . . . Worship, in a child, is to feel and practice love. [119]

IN THE HEART of a child who has grown up in spiritual unity with his parents, and is familiar with his own conscience, religious sentiments spring up sponta-neously. [120]

CHILDREN'S GARDEN WORK teaches them that the growth of plants does not depend on them, or on human power, but that an invisible power governs it. This teaches them almost without words to find the Creator. Only a

slight suggestion is needed to awaken the heart of the
child to love and thank the Giver of all good things. [121]

IF PARENTS DESIRE to give their children, as the
highest good in life, a firm hold on this never-failing
support, their union with those children must be both
real and evident wherever in prayer – be it in the home
or in the open fields – they acknowledge the common
and unifying fatherhood of God. Let it not be said that
the children do not grasp this unity; that is to deny
their highest life. . . . They grasp it not in thought but in
feeling. [122]

A RELIGIOUS SPIRIT thus fostered and nursed from
infancy will rise supreme in all storms and dangers of life.
This is the fruit of the earliest example on the part of the
parents, even when the child does not seem to notice it
or to understand it. Indeed, this is the case with all living
parental example. [123]

CAN YOU TELL when the spiritual development of
your child begins? Can you trace the boundary line that
separates the conscious from the unconscious soul? In
God's world, just because it is God's world, the law of
all things is continuity; there are and can be no abrupt

beginnings, no rude transitions, no today which is not based upon yesterday. The distant stars were shining long before their rays reached our earth; the seed germinates in darkness and is growing, long before we can see its growth; so in the depths of an infant's soul a process goes on which is hidden from our ken, yet upon which hangs more than we can dream of good or evil, happiness or misery. [124]

TEACH THE CHILD to pray, and also what are the claims and commands of the heavenly Father upon the child, and conscience awakens. Then direct the child's attention to the Christ Child. [125]

A CHILD should learn by heart prayers and Bible passages about the relation of people and nature to God. These show, as in a mirror, the child's own feelings, intuitions, and yearnings, and so confirm and strengthen them. [126]

CHILDREN APPROACH the outer world, with the feeling and hope and belief that it, too, is animated and ruled by a spirit like that which animates and rules them. And they are filled with an intense, irresistible longing, which returns with every new spring and every new fall, with every new, fresh morning and calm evening, with every peaceful festive day – a longing to know this all-ruling spirit, to make it their own. [127]

BY POINTING OUT God's works while rambling through the scenes of nature, a thousand opportunities offer for worship. [128]

Building Character

TO BE AN IMAGE OF GOD should be a man's highest aim in all his thoughts and actions, particularly when he stands in the relationship of a father to his children as God does to humans. In educating our children we should bear in mind that God's kingdom is of the spirit. . . . For this reason, we should concentrate on the general training of the human spirit in its proper sense – as an individual manifestation of the divine – confident that everyone who has been rightly educated as a human being is trained for all the demands and needs of civil and social life. [129]

AS EARLY AS POSSIBLE, let your child have the experience that what is good must be protected. The knowledge that you value and guard what is good will make the child's heart rejoice. [130]

THE MOST ACTIVE and influential force in the education of your children is your own true character. What you really are in yourself; what you really think about the disposition, deeds, and aims of your children; what you really approve and condemn; why you approve and why you condemn; what you prize and why you prize it; how you guard and cherish the things you prize – in a word, what you show yourself to be in yourself, in your home, and to your family – this is the power which will most influence your children, and that even when they are so small that you may imagine them incapable of understanding or even feeling it. [131]

IF YOU HAVE GIVEN your little children an abiding impression of the difference between straight and crooked, of dreariness in the feeling of crookedness, and of comfort in the feeling of straightness in action and life, in thought and speech, then directness and all that goes along with it will be the mark of all they do, and they will move free and joyfully in the right use of their well-developed strength in whatever is the right place for their working and activity. [132]

A CHILD WILL LEARN the great lesson of life . . . that he is both a free being and a dependent being. In a word, he will come to understand that a great Power reigns in the universe, and that this great Power gives and creates true freedom.

With premonition of this truth the child begins to care about what his elders think of him. When he attains this stage of development, then, parents, it is in your power to lead him in the path of right. You may allure him to so love the good that he will turn away instinctively even from evil thoughts. A new power or organ is sprouting within him. It seems at times like a voice, at times like an ear. It teaches him what is right and good. It warns him to avoid the bad. Through this germinating power you may incline him, if you will, toward all that is pure and righteous. Teach him to consider and follow what is right in his own deeds. Teach him to recognize and honor the good in others. By such watchful guidance you may help him to love, revere, and obey this inner power, even before he knows its name. [133]

INDEED, HEALTH, blessing, peace, and gladness are assured to children for whom, through their whole lives, the quiet call of conscience is the presentiment of that union of soul and spirit that is communion with the Highest, never again to be separated in feeling and consciousness. [134]

AS CHILDREN OF NATURE, humans are imprisoned, fettered beings, without self-mastery, under the dominion of their passions. As children of God, they become free agents, destined to self-mastery of their own free will, and hearing, conforming spiritual beings. [135]

THE WILL is strengthened only by voluntary activity. [136]

THE CHILD who learns to think will also work hard. This precept needs to be borne in mind by those of us who let our children become aimless and inactive. [137]

THE FACT that boys can be mischievous in school is no contradiction. The school should stimulate them to greater freedom; they ought to be full of life and vigor in both mind and body, and it may be that in their high spirits they will forget the possible consequences of their actions. [138]

THE SEASONS COME AND GO as regularly as the times of day: Spring, with its tide of new growth and wealth of blossoms, fills people (even in childhood) with gladness and new life; the blood flows faster and the heart beats louder. Autumn, with its falling brilliant and fragrant leaves, fills people (even as children) with a sense of longing and hope. And rigid but clear and steady, winter awakens courage and vigor; and these feelings of courage, vigor, perseverance, and renunciation fill the child's soul with a sense of freedom and joy. The joy with which children greet the first flowers and birds of spring is scarcely as jubilant as that with which they hail the first snowflakes that promise to their vigor and courage a smooth, quick road on which to fly to the distant goal.

All these things are presentiments of later life – hieroglyphics of a still life slumbering as yet in the soul; rightly understood, they are angels that guide a person through life. [139]

CHILDREN ARE GLAD to find phrases, especially in song, which give expression to emotions such as their joy in springtime or their sense of power, which they are not yet old or experienced enough to put into their own words. Cheerful and happy children love to sing, for in their songs they feels themselves really alive and express their sense of growing power as they wander through the valley and over the hill. [140]

CHILDREN IN THEIR PLAY seek out that which presents difficulty and struggle. [141]

THE HEALTHY BOY who has been brought up simply and naturally in childhood never shirks an obstacle or evades a difficulty. Rather, he seeks them that he may overcome them. "Let it be," cries the vigorous lad to his father who is about to take a log out of his way, "I can get over it." It may be that the first time he does it with difficulty, but he does it without help. With augmented strength and courage he returns and climbs the log again and again, till at length he leaps it easily, as if, indeed, there were no such obstacle in his way. [142]

BOYS ARE DARING and love adventure. They enjoy exploring caves and gorges, climbing trees and rocks, searching heights and depths, roaming through fields and forests. To a boy nothing seems difficult, nothing dangerous, so long as the impulse to do it springs from his own inner life of heart and will. But it is not only the impulse to put forth and test his strength which thus urges the boy abroad to hill and dale. Even more, it is the growing need of his spiritual life showing itself in an impulse to see many things, and to see them as parts of a whole; especially to bring the remote near to himself, to understand the range, the variety, the connectedness of all things – in a word, to extend his mental horizon. [143]

THE CLIMBING of a new tree is to the boy the discovery
of a new world. Seen from above, everything looks
quite different than it does when seen crowded and
foreshortened, on the level. If we could recall the feelings
that widened our soul and heart when as boys we saw the
narrowing bounds of common view disappear, we should
not so coldly call out to him, "Come down: you will fall!"
Ought we not – do we not – wish to give the boy this
uplifting of spirit and mind once in a while? Shall he not,
on sunlit height, clear his vision, widen his heart, by a look
into distance? "But the boy will be reckless; I shall never
have a moment's peace about him." The boy, who from
his first years has been led to use his strength as it grew,
will each time expect from himself just a little more than
he has already, and thus, as though led by a protecting
genius, will come safely through all dangers. 144

THE BOY who does not know his strength and the
demands made on it is likely to venture beyond his
experience and run into unsuspected danger. Those
boys are always the most reckless who have no constant
experience of their strength and suddenly have a burst
of energy when there is an opportunity to use it. Then
they are likely to run into danger, especially if anyone is
watching them. 145

SCHOOL-AGE CHILDREN should have some definite domestic duties to perform. They might even receive regular instruction from mechanics or farmers, such as has been frequently given by fathers inspired by vigorous and active natural insight. Especially should older children frequently be set by parents and teachers to doing things independently and alone (that is, errands), so that they may attain firmness and the art of self-examination in their actions. It is very desirable that such children should devote daily at least one or two hours to some definite external pursuit, some externally productive work. It is surely one of the greatest faults of our current school arrangements, especially of the so-called high schools, that the pupils are wholly debarred from outwardly productive work. [146]

DUTIES ARE NOT BURDENS but privileges. The fulfilment of duty strengthens body and soul. The sense of duty done gives self-reliance. [147]

IN A CHILD who has been overexcited by excess of food, either too much or too rich, may often be seen desires of a low kind. . . . If parents would consider how much future personal advantage to their children, domestic happiness, and even civic well-being would flow [from a healthy diet] how differently they would act! But in one case the mother is foolish, in another the father is weak; and we see poison upon poison given to children, in all shapes and ways, coarse and fine. On the one hand, it is oppressive quantity: the continual giving of food, leaving the body no time to digest, perhaps feeding just to drive away the boredom which comes of want of occupation. On the other, it is food of too luxurious a quality, which only stimulates the physical life without contributing to mental or other higher vitality, and thus acts to weaken and wear out the body. Here, bodily laziness is looked on as a call for rest; there, restlessness, the result of physical overexcitement, is mistaken for genuine liveliness of spirit. [148]

LET THE CHILD'S FOOD be strictly the means of nourishment, with the one object of securing activity of body and mind. Never allow food, or the quality, flavor, or delicacy of food, to become an end to be sought for its own sakes. See, then, that every child's food be as simple and plain as circumstances permit, and that the amount given be proportioned to bodily and mental activity. [149]

CLOTHING MUST NOT be tight, or binding. Clothes – their shape, color, and fashion – must never appear an end in themselves, else they will soon draw children away from their true selves, making them vain and outward, dolls instead of children, puppets in place of human beings. Clothing is therefore by no means unimportant, either for the child or for the adult. [150]

AND ONE MUST ALWAYS watch out for this: that children who receive presents do not have their nature cramped and stunted by it. According to the measure of how much they receive, they should be able to give away. In fact, this is a necessity for simple-hearted children. Happy are those little ones who understand how to satisfy this need of their natures, to give by producing various gifts of their own creation! [151]

PROTECT THE NEW GENERATION: do not let them grow up into emptiness and nothingness, to the avoidance of good hard work, to introspection and analyzation without deeds, or to mechanical actions without thought and consideration. Guide the young away from the harmful chase after outer things and the damaging passion for distraction. [152]

3

At School

AN INSTITUTE OF EDUCATION should have the character of a family. [153]

IT WOULD BE WELL for our children and for future generations if we realized that we possess a great load of extraneous knowledge, which has been imposed on us and which we foolishly strive daily to increase, and that we have very little knowledge of our own that has originated in our own mind and grown with it. We must not pride ourselves on thoughts and feelings that are not our own. We must cease to estimate the success of our education and our schools in terms of this show of knowledge. [154]

MY EXPERIENCES, especially those of my university career, had taught me quite unequivocally that existing

educational methods, especially if mere instruction
or the communication of external facts and historical
explanations was the aim, blunted – I might even say
destroyed – any attempt in the schools to promote true
knowledge or give any genuine scientific training. It was
my firm conviction, which I still hold, that the entire
system of instruction, even that part of it which had been
improved, should be radically revised and the emphasis
placed on creation and growth. What I really wanted was
the complete antithesis of everything then done in the
way of education and instruction. [155]

ONCE AGAIN I found myself in conflict with my
environment; for I could not possibly torture my
students with what I myself had refused to be tortured
with – namely, the learning by heart of disconnected
rules. I was therefore compelled to strike out fresh paths
for myself, which indeed my post rendered a delightful
task, because I not only had full liberty accorded me in
this matter but was even urged onward in that direction
by my duty, since the institution was a model school for
the higher development of teaching. My past self-culture,
self-teaching, and self-development and my study of
nature and of life now stood me in good stead. [156]

The Purpose of School

TO STIR UP, to animate, to awaken, and to strengthen
the pleasure and power of the human being to labor
uninterruptedly at their own education, has become and
always remained the fundamental principle and aim of
my educational work. [157]

CHILDREN ENTER SCHOOL with the hope that here
they will be taught something which they cannot learn
elsewhere, that here the hunger of their mind and heart
will be satisfied. [158]

I WANTED to educate people to be free, to think, and to
be self-motivated. [159]

IT IS THE FIRST and most important task of all
elementary education to awaken in the pupils not only
their innate ability but also that spontaneous drive and
keenness which is fundamental to reflection and thought.
This drive is easily aroused if total and free development
is permitted. [160]

NEVER SHOULD IT BE FORGOTTEN that the work of
the school is less to teach many things than to bring out
clearly the essential unity of all things. [161]

ABOVE ALL there should be special regard for the care of nature and for creativity and representation in material form. [162]

IT IS NOT the getting of a greater or lesser amount of varied knowledge that makes a school, but the living spirit which animates all things – a point which all those who direct or manage schools should keep in mind. [163]

The Role of Sports

PHYSICAL GAMES have a special place in educational institutions, for the pupil must be trained in physical skill as well as in strength and endurance. It is not to be supposed that a child who works hard physically does not need such free activity or that, since so much physical work goes on, no organized physical exercises are useful. [164]

A DEXTEROUS AND VIGOROUS BODY, competent to meet all the demands of life, and a dignified carriage, are produced only by a general training of the body as officer of the mind. Giving children systematic bodily training, adapted to their mental development and advancing from simple to complex exercises, would do much to lessen rudeness, coarseness, and awkwardness of manners. In childhood the will does not have constant control of the body; consequently, the body should be trained to carry out automatically the intentions of the mind, as we see in the case of a skilled musician. Without such cultivation of the body, education can never attain its end of complete human development. So the body as well as the mind should receive an all-round training, and physical education should be given by every school.

Without this, real discipline, which is the very center of education, is impossible. Discipline implies that the children in all their actions respect their own human nature because they realize its dignity and worth. The more clearly they recognize the requirements of their true humanity, the more definitely and firmly should the educator insist on the fulfilment of those requirements. [165]

I STUDIED THE BOYS' PLAY, the whole series of games in the open air, and learned to recognize their mighty power to awaken and to strengthen the intelligence and the soul as well as the body. In these games and what was connected with them I detected the mainspring of the moral strength that animated the children in the institution. The games, as I am now fervently assured, formed a mental bath of extraordinarily strengthening power, and although the sense of the higher symbolic meaning of games had not yet dawned upon me, I was nevertheless able to perceive in each boy genuinely at play a moral strength governing both mind and body which won my highest esteem. [166]

THE GAMES OF CHILDHOOD are, or ought to be, pure results of the child's spirit, strength, and life, engendered by the fullness of life and joy that stirs within the child. [167]

MANY GAMES HAVE as their object simply to test and display strength. But, whatever its nature, the play shows the characteristic feature of childhood – the presence of definite conscious purpose. This appears more and more plainly with each passing year, and is evident even in such games as running, racing, boxing, wrestling, games of hunting, sham fights, games with balls. [168]

A SENSE OF GROWING POWER makes such games so delightful to a child. Nor is it only bodily power that is fed and strengthened by them; moral and intellectual vigor is also fostered and concentrated. Indeed, the spiritual life gains more than the physical life. Justice, temperance, self-control, truth, faithfulness, brotherly love, strict impartiality, are all to be seen in a group of boys playing such games; to say nothing of courage, endurance, determination, coolness, and the banishment

of slackness and self-indulgence, and those other fruits of
a good heart and a firm will – forbearance, patience, care
for the weak. [169]

EVERY TOWN AND VILLAGE should provide a special
playground for its children. Rich would be its reward!
For, whenever they can, children play together, and so
their games cultivate the sense of common interests
and social obligations. The child seeks to see and feel
himself in his companions, to pit himself against them
and measure himself by them, and so to know himself
through them. So it is that games develop social and civic
virtues, and thus train the boy for life. [170]

Storytelling

A GOOD STORYTELLER is a precious boon. Blessed is
the circle of children that can enjoy him; his influence
is great and ennobling; the more so, the less he seems to
aim at this. With high esteem and full of respect I greet
a genuine storyteller; with intense gratitude I grasp him
by the hand. However, better greeting than mine is his
lot; behold the joyful faces, the sparkling eyes, the merry
shouts that welcome him; see the blooming circle of
delighted children crowd around him, like a wreath of
fresh flowers and branches around the bard of joy and
delight! [171]

WHO FAILS TO REMEMBER the keen desire that
filled the heart, more particularly in the later years of
childhood, when beholding old walls and towers on hills
and on the roadside – to hear others give accounts of
these things, of their time and their causes? Who has not
at such times noticed a vague, undefinable feeling that at
some time these things themselves could and would give
an account of themselves and their time?

And who, judging by experience and knowledge, can
furnish these accounts, if not those who lived before – the
elders? That these might tell us is our earnest wish; and
thus there develops in children the desire and craving
for tales, legends, and all kinds of stories, and later on
for historical accounts. This craving, especially in its first
appearance, is very intense; so much so, that, when others
fail to gratify it, the children seek to gratify it themselves,
particularly on days of leisure, and in times when the
regular employments of the day are ended.

Who has not been filled with respect when noticing
a group of children gathered around one whom a good
memory and a lively imagination have designated as their
storyteller? How attentively they all listen when his story
gratifies their favorite wish and confirms their judgment
by its plot and incidents – in short, when it brings before
them words and deeds in harmony with their own
thoughts and feelings! [172]

CHILDREN ARE ATTRACTED to the legend and fairy tale, not by the varied and colorful forms that move about in them, but by their spiritual life, which furnishes children with a measure for their own life and spirit. [173]

THOUGH THE STORY may present strange people and strange lands, other times and other manners, yet in it the hearer seeks and finds an image of himself, even if no one else could say, "That is like you." [174]

THIS IS THE CHIEF REASON why children are so fond of stories, legends, and tales; the more so when these are told as having actually occurred at some time, or as lying within the reach of probability, for which, however, there are scarcely any limits for a child.

The power that has scarcely germinated in children's minds is seen by them in the legend or tale, a perfect plant filled with the most delicious blossoms and fruits. The very remoteness of the comparison with their own vague hopes expands heart and soul, strengthens the mind, unfolds life in freedom and power. [175]

NO EXPLICIT MORAL need be drawn, no practical application made. The life itself as told makes a deeper impression if left to speak for itself. For who can say exactly what were the young hearer's spiritual needs? [176]

The Teacher's Task

THE PURPOSE OF TEACHING and instruction is to bring the best out of a person rather than to put more and more into him. [177]

WE DO NOT ALLOW even a fine young person who has the best intentions to work independently as a teacher. They may have youthful enthusiasm and courage, but they have not yet been tested, nor have they tested themself to see if teaching is their vocation. God puts even his chosen teachers through difficult trials and educates them himself, as it were, before he entrusts the dear children to them for their schooling. Mortals are often too sure of themselves, they tend to look outside rather than inside themselves, and depend on the sensual rather than the spiritual. Therefore, God puts those teachers whom he has appointed through continuous testing even while they are teaching. He teaches them to be quiet and follow his leading. [178]

TEACHING SHOULD always be in answer to a need really felt by the child. [179]

THE TEACHER'S FUNCTION is to point out and make intelligible the nature of things. This is what every pupil expects of his teacher, and this expectation forms an invisible but potent bond between them. [180]

WE DO NOT TEACH simply for an outer goal, let alone a personal objective, no matter what name you give it. We teach purely so that the child can unfold and develop into the person God created; so they will be honest, hardworking, knowledgeable, and resourceful in whatever occupation or location God and fate have placed them. That is why teaching is not a line of business, like forestry or beekeeping. Instead, we consider it a freer, truer, deeper profession. [181]

DO NOT ANSWER in words, where it can answer itself, without your word. Easier it is, to be sure, to hear – perhaps only half hear, and half understand – an answer, than to look for, and find it, for oneself. [182]

IF YOU WISH your instruction to be natural and impressive, begin by giving concrete experiences. Do you ask why this method is impressive and why its results are abiding? I answer: that which we have ourselves experienced makes a deep impression. [183]

THE EDUCATOR must also take into account children's propensity to copy in their own lives the role models set before them, and this is the greatest and most effective means of influencing them. [184]

IT CANNOT ALWAYS be demonstrated with certainty that the inner spirit of a child has been injured; at least it is difficult to discover the source and tendency of the injury. . . . Because of this uncertainty in evaluation, education should be far more supportive and following, than directional and prescriptive. [185]

BE GUIDED by children's questions, for they will teach you, and they will not be content with half-truths. [186]

IF YOU FOLLOW children's questions both you and they will learn from them. It is true that children ask questions that no one can answer. Either they take you to the limit of earthly knowledge and the threshold of the divine – in which case you should tell the child and he will be satisfied in his mind – or they merely surpass your own knowledge and experience, and this you must admit, being careful not to speak as if the limits of your knowledge were those of humankind's, for this would stunt their mind's growth. You and they must seek to understand the problem together and find an answer . . . for you will see God clearly revealed in all his works. [187]

BETWEEN THE EDUCATOR and pupil, between request and obedience, there should rule a third invisible thing to which educator and pupil are equally subject – the right, the best. The recognition of, and obedience to, the rule of this third thing should be constantly and clearly evident in the bearing and conduct of the teacher. The child has a very keen feeling, a very clear apprehension, and rarely fails to distinguish whether what the parent or teacher says is personal and arbitrary, or whether it is an objective truth and necessity.

In all education it should be irrefutably clear that the one who makes the demand is himself strictly subject to an eternally ruling law. . . . This obedience, this trustful yielding to an unchangeable third principle by both pupil and teacher, should be present in even the smallest details. [188]

TEACHING AND LEARNING go on all through life. Even the oldest teacher has something to learn, and the oldest educators must let themselves be taught – not by people alone but by everything around them, and even by the animals. [189]

CHILDREN – FRESH IN SPIRIT, cheerful in mood, joyous in soul, happy in life – have usually surrounded me while I write, playing close by, never tired of demanding fresh satisfaction and nourishment for their impulses to life and activity, providing assurance that what I have written is true. [190]

Bibliography

AUTOBIOGRAPHY

Froebel, Friedrich. *Autobiography of Friedrich Froebel.* Translated and edited
by Emilie Michaelis and H. Keatley Moore. Syracuse: C. W.
Bardeen, 1889.

CHAPIN

Chapin, Fanny, ed. *Friedrich Froebel Yearbook: Compiled from the Writings of
Friedrich Froebel.* Chicago: Kindergarten Literature Co., 1894.

DWIGHT

Froebel, Friedrich. *Mother-Play and Nursery Songs: Poetry, Music and Pictures
for the Noble Culture of Child Life with Notes to Mothers.* Translated
from the German by Fannie E. Dwight and Josephine Jarvis;
edited by Elizabeth P. Peabody. 1898. Reprint. Middletown, DE,
University of Michigan Library, 2018.

ELIOT

Eliot, Henrietta R, and Blow, Susan E. *The Mottoes and Commentaries of
Friedrich Froebel's Mother Play.* New York: D. Appleton and
Company, 1895. Reprint. Miami: HardPress Publishing.

ERNING

Erning, Günter. *Umschrift der Mutter- und Koselieder von Friedrich Fröbel.*
Universitat Bamberg, 2011.

FLETCHER

Fletcher, S. S. F, and J. Welton, trans. *Froebel's Chief Writings on Education.*
New York: Longmans, Green & Co.; London: Edward Arnold,
1912.

HAILMANN

Froebel, Friedrich. *The Education of Man.* Translated and annotated by W. N.
Hailmann. 1887.

HAYWARD

Hayward, F. H. *The Educational Ideas of Pestalozzi and Froebel.* London:
Ralph Holland and Co., 1904.

HEINEMANN

Heinemann, Arnold H., ed. *Froebel Letters.* Boston: Lee and Shepard
Publishers, 1893.

HERFORD, VOL. I

Herford, Willian H., ed. *The Student's Froebel, adapted from Die Menschenerziehung. Part I: Theory of Education.* Boston: D.C. Heath & Co., 1896.

HERFORD, VOL. II

Herford, Willian H., ed. *The Student's Froebel, adapted from Die Menschenerziehung of F. Froebel. Part II: Practice of Education.* London: Sir Isaac Pitman and Sons, Ltd., 1905.

HUGHES

Hughes, James L. Froebel's Educational Laws for All Teachers. New York: D. Appleton and Company, 1897.

LANGE

Lange, Wichard. *Friedrich Fröbel's gesammelte pädagogische Schriften.* Erste Abtheilung: Friedrich Fröbel in seiner Entwicklung als Mensch und Pädagog. Erster Band: Autobiographie und kleinere Schriften. Berlin: Verlag von Th. Chr. Fr. Enslin, 1862.

LILLEY

Lilley, Irene M. *Friedrich Froebel: A Selection from His Writings.* Cambridge: University Press, 1967.

LORD

Lord, Frances, and Emily Lord, trans. *Mother's Songs, Games and Stories. Fröbel's "Mutter- und Kose-Lieder."* London: William Rice, 1888.

MARENHOLTZ

Marenholtz-Bülow, Bertha von. *Reminiscences of Friedrich Froebel.* Translated by Mrs. Horace Mann. With a sketch of the life of Friedrich Froebel by Emily Shirreff. Honolulu: University Press of the Pacific, 2004.

MICHAELIS

Michaelis, Emilie, and H. Keatley Moore, trans., ed., annotated. *Froebel's Letters on the Kindergarten: Translated from the German Edition of 1887 by Hermann Poesche.* Syracuse, NY: C. W. Bardeen, Publisher, 1896.

POULSON

Poulson, Emilie. *Finger Plays for Nursery and Kindergarten.* New York, NY: Dover Publications, 1971.

Notes

1. Lilley, 92
2. Hailmann, 20
3. Chapin, 89
4. Hailmann, 15–16
5. Lilley, 95
6. Herford vol. I, 5
7. Eliot, 57–58, paraphrased
8. Hailmann, 21
9. Michaelis, 267
10. Chapin, 116
11. Hailmann, 23–24
12. Herford vol. I, 12
13. Lilley, 75
14. Hailmann, 29
15. Hailmann, 30
16. Fletcher, 21
17. Lilley, 87
18. Herford vol. I, 12
19. Eliot, 306
20. Fletcher, 40
21. Chapin, 121
22. Hayward, 67
23. Herford vol. I, 103–104
24. Hailmann, 9
25. Chapin, 63
26. Hughes, 228
27. Hailmann, 34
28. Hailmann, 86
29. Lilley, 135
30. Fletcher, 77
31. Fletcher, 76
32. Lilley, 51
33. Fletcher, 92
34. Hailmann, 310
35. Hailmann, 309
36. Fletcher, 110

37. Hailmann, 173
38. Chapin, 78
39. Fletcher, 50
40. Lilley, 148–149
41. Lilley, 149
42. Fletcher, 100–101
43. Eliot, 303
44. Hailman, 312
45. Fletcher, 101
46. Lilley, 128–129
47. Lilley, 127
48. Lord, 166
49. Fletcher, 31
50. Lilley, 94
51. Hailmann, 13
52. Hailmann, 142
53. Hailmann, 32–33
54. Hailmann, 105–106
55. Lilley, 128
56. Lilley, 97
57. Lilley, 94
58. Lilley, 157
59. Hailmann, 30
60. Lilley, 65
61. Chapin, 131
62. Hailmann, 79
63. Hailmann, 75
64. Lilley, 130
65. Lilley, 114
66. Lilley, 94
67. Lilley, 155
68. Marenholtz, 103–104, editor's translation
69. Lilley 83–84
70. Lilley, 84
71. Lilley, 106
72. Marenholtz, 67, editor's translation
73. Franks, 135–136
74. Hailmann, 111
75. Lilley, 167
76. Poulson, 5

77. Hailmann, 303
78. Eliot, 127
79. Chapin, 79
80. Erning, 107–108, editor's translation
81. Autobiography, 104
82. Autobiography, 69
83. Lilley, 123
84. Michaelis, 273
85. Eliot, 218
86. Lilley, 79
87. Lilley, 74–75
88. Lilley, 58–59
89. Fletcher, 87–88
90. Herford vol. I, 11
91. Hailmann, 16–17
92. Lilley, 75
93. Lilley, 114
94. Heinemann, 71
95. Marenholtz, 155–156, editor's translation
96. Chapin, 16
97. Eliot, 229
98. Hailmann, 25–26
99. Hailmann, 42
100. Hailmann, 49
101. Lilley, 76–77
102. Lilley, 78
103. Lilley, 77
104. Fletcher, 53
105. Eliot, 227
106. Hailmann, 71–72
107. Hailmann, 73–74
108. Hailmann, 54
109. Lilley, 76
110. Hailmann, 79
111. Herford vol. I, 37–38
112. Lilley, 123–124
113. Herford vol. I, 53
114. Herford vol. I, 53
115. Chapin, 46
116. Chapin, 139

117. Fletcher, 89
118. Lilley, 62
119. Marenholtz, 189–190, editor's translation
120. Fletcher, 93
121. Chapin, 122
122. Fletcher, 40
123. Hailmann, 26–27
124. Chapin, 26
125. Chapin, 187
126. Fletcher, 83
127. Chapin, 69
128. Hughes, 268
129. Lilley, 157–158
130. Eliot, 305
131. Eliot, 251
132. Lord, 145
133. Eliot, 314–315
134. Dwight, 190
135. Chapin, 11
136. Hughes, 100
137. Lilley, 90–91
138. Lilley, 138
139. Hailmann, 265–266
140. Lilley, 131–132
141. Lilley, 132
142. Fletcher, 68
143. Fletcher, 68–69
144. Herford vol. I, 54–55
145. Lilley, 126–127
146. Hailmann, 236
147. Eliot, 201
148. Herford I, 32–33
149. Fletcher, 51
150. Herford vol. I, 34
151. Autobiography, 77
152. Inscription in the Barop tower, Bad Blankenburg, Germany.
153. Chapin, 45
154. Lilley, 156
155. Lilley, 41–42
156. Autobiography, 109–110

157. Hughes, 100
158. Lilley, 138
159. Lilley, 41
160. Lilley, 164
161. Fletcher, 80-81
162. Lilley, 161
163. Lilley, 137
164. Lilley, 168
165. Fletcher, 95
166. Autobiography, 82
167. Herford vol. II, 74
168. Fletcher, 71
169. Fletcher, 71
170. Fletcher, 71–72
171. Chapin, 129–130
172. Hailmann, 115–116
173. Hailmann, 306
174. Fletcher, 149
175. Hailmann, 306
176. Fletcher, 150
177. Hughes, 98
178. Lange, 356, editor's translation
179. Lilley, 153
180. Lilley, 137
181. Lange, S. 355–356, editor's translation
182. Herford vol. I, 44
183. Eliot, 122
184. Lilley, 166
185. Hailmann, 10
186. Fletcher, 110
187. Lilley, 149
188. Hailmann, 14–15
189. Lord, 156–157
190. Herford vol. I, 108

Related Titles from Plough

Children's Education in Community
The Basis of Bruderhof Education
Eberhard Arnold

Thoughts on Children
Christoph F. Blumhardt and Johann C. Blumhardt

Their Name Is Today
Reclaiming Childhood in a Hostile World
Johann Christoph Arnold

Why Children Matter
Johann Christoph Arnold

The Liberating Arts
Why We Need Liberal Arts Education
Edited by Jeffrey Bilbro, Jessica Hooten Wilson
and David Henreckson

Plough Publishing House
845-572-3455 ✦ info@plough.com
PO BOX 398, Walden, NY 12586, USA
Robertsbridge, East Sussex TN32 5DR, UK
4188 Gwydir Highway, Elsmore, NSW 2360, Australia
www.plough.com

Printed in the USA
CPSIA information can be obtained
at www.ICGtesting.com
JSHW081741230724
66917JS00003B/154